Crazy
Chicana
in Catholic City

Crazy
Chicana
in Catholic City

Poems

JULIANA ARAGÓN FATULA

AN IMPRINT OF BOWER HOUSE
DENVER

Library of Congress Cataloging-in-Publication Data is available
upon request.

ISBN 978-0-9713678-4-5

10 9 8 7 6 5 4 3 2 1

ACKNOWLEDGMENTS

Some of the poems in this book appeared as earlier versions in the following journals and anthologies:

Open Windows III: "Bloody Cookies," Ghost Road Press

El Tecolote: "Myth of the Boogey Man"

The Hungry Eye Literary Magazine: "A Real American Hero," "rage," "el día de los muertos," and "Two Spirit"

Southern Colorado Women's Poetry Series Volume VII: "Black Bridge," "Colorado Sisters," and "Bilateral Mammogram Dx Rx Right Breast Asymmetry"

Some poems appear at *The Hispanic Cultural Experience* 2007 and 2008 at colostate-pueblo.edu/hispanicexperience

"At Wind River" appears at the Wind River Ranch, New Mexico at windriverranch.org

At first I thought I was very lucky, now I know I am very blessed. I wish to express my heartfelt thanks to Dan R. McDaniel, Vincent Fatula, Tracy Harmon, Maria Melendez, Sandra Cisneros and the Macondistas, Jimmy Santiago Baca, Lorna Dee Cervantes, David Keplinger, Juan Morales, Daniel Olivas, Linda Rodriguez, Aimee Medina Carr, El Centro Su Teatro, Colorado State University-Pueblo. This edition is the result of dedication by Sonya Unrein to see her work to fruition. When she moved to Conundrum Press she brought me with her. I am so grateful to both Sonya Unrein and Caleb Seeling for bringing my book back to print.

And to las mujeres (you know who you are) who always had my back.

Contents

LAS MUJERES

LOS HOMBRES

GARDEN OF EDEN

For Peachie—

*a Colorado sister, mother, grandmother,
great-grandmother, and great-great-grandmother,
a Crazy Chicana in Catholic City.*

Preface

A woman of color who writes poetry or paints or dances or makes
movies knows there is no escape from race or gender when she
is writing or painting. She can't take off her color and sex and
leave them at the door....nor can she leave behind her history.
Art is about identity, among other things, and her creativity is
political...creative acts are forms of political activism....

—Gloria Anzaldúa, Editor
Making Faces Making Soul

I am a performance artist who writes poetry. When I am on stage reading my poems, I feel euphoric. My original audience in Denver at El Centro Su Teatro was mainly Chicano/a. At the Mercury Café, my audience was filled with feminists, Native Americans, and old hippies. So, I suppose my poems appeal to Spanglish speaking, feminist, hippy, liberals. I like to say, "I've had a good reading when I can make the men cry and the women laugh." I have become a storyteller, a healer, a curendera for the soul.

I used to walk among all of the books in the public library and imagine my book on the shelf. I wanted to leave something behind, my herstory, and as a writer, I can share my culture, language, my truth. Today, my book is in several libraries throughout the country.

I moved from Denver to Southern Colorado in 1998, to be near my mother. My mother and I spent the last ten years of her life laughing, crying, and sharing stories. These stories morphed into the poetry in *Crazy Chicana in Catholic City*. Some of my poems arose from a need to purge myself of all of the black secrets that were consuming me. My style of confessional poetry stems from my desire to tell my story and in doing so aid others who are survivors.

The book began in writing workshops at Colorado State University–Pueblo in 2004 and over the next few years of creative writing courses, I accumulated enough poems to submit a manuscript for publishing. On advice of my professor, David Keplinger, I submitted my work to a publisher and one year later my book hit the shelves.

The book is divided into three sections: Las Mujeres, Los Hombres, and the Garden of Eden. The first poem begins with a story about grandmother and her grandson who is a drug addict, and ends with a poem about my ancestors and their sacrifices for their children. I am the grandmother, the drug addict, the ancestors, and the children. My Cocoman, la Llorona, el diablo, el Cui Cui, became characters representing my dark side. In several poems, drowning is prevalent: la Llorona drowns her children, young teens are saved from drowning in the muddy river by a drug addict, the young Chicana daydreams of suicide by drowning, like Shakespeare's Ophelia. But also the moon and stars represent the Chicana rising—shining, succeeding. And because of my twisted sense of humor, I blend chaos and calm: drag queens, priests, heathens, and lunatics. They are all based on people I know and love.

Writing has become my sweet medicine. I hope to write until someone pries the pen from my dying carcass.

—Juliana Aragón Fatula, April 18, 2012

I will no longer be made to feel ashamed of existing. I will have my voice: Indian, Spanish, White. I will have my serpent's tongue— my woman's voice, my sexual voice, my poet's voice. I will overcome the tradition of silence.

—Gloria Anzaldúa

From *Borderlands/La Frontera: The New Mestiza*

A Real American Hero

I met my grandson
when he was twelve months old.
His mother was fourteen.
He was born in San Francisco.
He's dark like me
but his hair is lighter than mine,
like the color of clay
here on the rez.

He's an earth boy with eyes full of earth.
When my grandson laughs,
it's like rain in the desert.
He never met a stranger:
smiled with his eyes.

When he was five years old
he stood in front of the house
and asked everyone
who passed by for a nickel.
He panhandled all day
and had big plans.

He could swim upstream
like a rainbow trout,
with arms like fins,
legs swift and mean.
As a teen he swam
in the muddy river all summer.
Every year some kid would drown;
he saved some of 'em.
He was a hero,
saved people all the time.

In high school,
he'd sit in the park and ask everyone
who walked by, "Wanna get high?"
He sold enough weed
to buy a one-way ticket
back to San Francisco.
He went looking for his father,
said he was gonna'
kick his dad's ass,
but he didn't.
He got drunk with him instead.

His father took
off his belt one day,
wrapped it tight around my
grandson's bicep and
punched the needle in his veins.
My grandson burns his track marks
with a hot iron
to brand himself with shame.
He's full of scars.

We prayed for rain.
He came home one day.
looking old, old like a dog.
He threw his arms around my neck
so gently; he looked deep into my eyes
for a long time.
Large nose, solid brow of clay,
carved in granite, mahogany, lava stone;
adorned with feathers, white fox, deer horns,
leather and beads. Aztec, Mayan, Anasazi.
He looks out of the cosmos,
dances through the waves,
the fire, the moon.

LAS MUJERES

Bloody Cookies

Nothing lives long, only the earth and the mountains.

—Cheyenne Death Song

Her first husband, the Bull,
broke her nose so bad
they couldn't fix it;
she looked like a retired boxer.
When mom left the Bull,
he knifed her in a parking lot,
stabbed her twelve times;

she was twenty-six.
He left her for dead.
She survived.
She's half-Apache;
half-warrior woman.
She comes from
a long-line of survivors.

My parents got drunk on weekends.
Mom battered Dad's ass. Dad let her.
She had a lot to be angry
about. He didn't mind if she took it out on him.
He was her human punching bag
and never raised a hand.
He was the most macho-feminist
I ever knew. She was a good wife and mother.

Mom was born in a shack with dirt floors,
built right next to the river.
She survived floods, hunger,
stab and gun wounds. She collected coal
from the train tracks to keep warm at
night. She ate her fishy-fish.

21

She ate suckers, fish that eat
the crap on the bottom of the river.
She looks like a goddess: pure white
hair; velvety dark skin like cocoa, not
one wrinkle. Eyes twinkle, twinkle,
twinkle, from all of the fish
and fish and fish.

•

Eighty-nine years-old, diabetic,
can hardly swallow, has a hard
time keeping food down, pees her pants
when she laughs, sneezes, gets
too excited, when she farts she shits
her pants. She wears diapers and eats
baby food. She wants cookies
for breakfast, lunch, and dinner.
What the hell; she's been shot, stabbed,
given birth to ten kids. Let her
have cookies.

•

Mom once took a bullet for a cookie.
Grandma had an apron full of cherries.
Auntie hung the wash.
Lee fed the chickens. Zeke
cleaned his rifle. Mom
searched the cupboards. She was only
three feet tall. She stood on the sink,
tried to reach high in the sky
for oatmeal cookies. *Crack* - like
a lightening bolt had hit a cottonwood
tree. Her blood was everywhere: on the
cupboards, floor, cookies, hands.

Grandma ran down the hill but she fell.
She rolled, she rolled, she rolled;
just like a tortilla. She ran in the house
saw Zeke had wrapped
mom's legs in torn sheets while mom
ate cookies. The bullet went in the left
leg, out the back, and through the right leg,
four holes, total. That's why you should never
clean a rifle in the house: bloody cookies.

The First Woman to See the Moon

She hid in light.
The first woman
to see the moon wept:
menses ran down her thigh.
La luna teased, seduced, glowed,
touched her darkness. Her tears,
the first tide, created the oceans.

Revenge

Asiatic Princess ignites
voracious impulses, fierce,
toxic, raw, sexual sparks.

Jason haunts her, the rancorous
monster bent on murder: King
Kreon, Glauke, her sons.

The sorceress poisons the bride,
ambivalence slays the children, horror
like fire flickers.

In her golden gossamer gown
eyes bulge, white frothy lips snarl,
decrepit flesh curdles,

blood spilt onto marble floors
sinks into the dark veins
of Medea, the lustful brute.

The Colorado Sisters

Grandma Peachie
Chicana – biker – cowgirl – chick – a legend,
sings, "If you get drunk, jito,
you'll get shit on your face."
Peachie and her sister,
Jesusita, were known
as the Colorado Sisters.
They liked whiskey.
They liked beer.
They liked wine.
In high heels, hats
and girdles they walked
to Bernie's on the Hill
with their friend, Rosalinda.

They shot some pool,
as they sang, *I Go Out Walking After Midnight*,
with the jukebox and Patsy Cline,
drank some Coors, *It's the water and a lot more.*
Closing time they stumbled,
crawled home. Rosalinda
said goodnight and just like pulling a conejo
out of a hat – disappeared.
Her father, siempre borracho,
had moved the outhouse and
forgot to cover up the old hole.
She slid and fell face first. She screamed,
"Aquí huele a pura cuchapeta y a pedo!
It smells like pussies and farts in here!"
In the dark hole glimmered
Rosalinda's pretty earrings.
They were the only thing
not covered in mierda.

The Colorado Sisters
pulled her out. They pumped
some well water.
They washed her face,
hair, and dress;
put her in a clean night gown
and stayed
until she fell asleep.
In white cotton with eyelet
lace trim she looked angelic
except for caca flecks
stuck in her ears and the fact:
that she was shitfaced.

yo soy la Llorona

The moon has nothing to be sad about, staring from her hood of bone.
She is used to this sort of thing. Her blacks crackle and drag.

From "Edge" — Sylvia Plath

My ten years grew heavy,
dark pain like la Llorona's rage.
My village called me spic, fag, squaw, ho.
Prayers are dangerous.
I begged for salvation. God sent
mysteries—gave me black
secrets. I threw myself
river parties: hoped for fast currents.
I sang opera for solutions.
I tried to die . . . to sleep—no more.

Black Bridge

She wears a blood-red suit.
Hair the color of screaming,
black. Her skin tan as a leather briefcase
holds secrets inside.

Under the cold steel bridge,
hiding in the quiet moonlight,
she shows her true self
in the river reflection.

Milkweed smells of caterpillars;
crying, la Llorona laughs in tune
with the clickety click of the slow train.
The ancestor dumps his old beer cans.
He stinks: cigarillos and Aqua Velvet.
His stomach makes noises like prayers.
Womens' and children's blood soaked into
Sand Creek. No more death, no more murder. Listen.
She baptizes in tears, thirty-year-old
memories, twelve mean kisses,
drunk breath of el tío, ice cream promises.
Water is cold, dark. Fourteen: floating
down river, pregnant, unwed, until caught
in the weeds, face down
as though she were Ophelia
drowned in defeat, whispers, and lies.

Baptismal Drowning

Poverty eats up souls.
Terror lies in children's hearts.
She plays with gringos on the streets,
sits at the river, and wonders
how long it would take to sink
to the black bottom like la Llorona's babies.

Mexican dirt drips down her face.
She prays on the edge of the current
flowing east; the amber sphere
vanishing in the west.
She prays for a reason not to slip
into the icy water.

He saves two lives,
God's seed miracle:
she feels her son kick
on her fourteenth birthday.

Her son in the womb
swims upstream,
fights the mud that clings like licorice,
learning to surf rough waters.
He saves lives and baptizes souls,
thumps his fists against their lungs,
sings life into their bodies.
This little dark man with cosmos eyes.
His heart vast as the ocean.

Petrified Hearts

His sweat smells of dead rivers,
wood and hunger, fire and winter,
storms of unspoken words.
The sharp ax splits the log
reveals the aspen heart
unborn, unseen.

It's smooth and clean, perfect,
a knot that grew into a tree.
Three knots to the beat taps the crux, the core.
The grain bleeds rose sandstone.
Hidden like the secret mummy in the tomb,
the spirit of the tree.

The wife kisses the mistake,
wraps it in leather,
prays it felt no pain.
The husband's smile a lie;
he'll never know the pain of birth,
the bleeding, the waste.

She thinks about the fetus pulled from her womb;
the smooth, sandy colored knot,
three heart beats pulsed and weakened.
Her heart petrified into wood.

The Truth

If you do not tell the truth about yourself, you cannot tell it about others.

—Virginia Woolf

I can't close my legs; my legs
are spread like I'm an old cowhand that's
ridden a few too many bulls. At night in bed,
I make my legs into a perfect
diamond shape. I sleep this way, only
the soles of my feet touch.

Ever since I got drunk,
fell through the black bridge,
broke my tail bone, (but didn't know
it) then fucked all night with the drummer
from that terrible blues band, I have not
been able to close my legs.

Truthfully, it goes further back than that,
back to when I was twelve; I opened my
legs for the first time for the neighbor, that
black Inuit boy from Anchorage, who had
eyes like two dead chunks of coal.

After that it was backseats, drive-ins, alleys,
bathroom stalls. I opened my legs and I
never shut them again. I let in stranger after
stranger, men who bought me drinks, lovers,
husbands who wanted to possess me. I let
them all in, spread my legs wide and gave it
away for free. Men bought me bouquets,
rings, TVs; but no one ever paid for it.

I've always had my legs open wide, even
way back that summer morning when I was
five; all my cousins and brothers
playing outside, all except for Joey and me.
I spread my legs for Joey;
he gave me ice cream,
told me it's our secret. No
wonder I can't close my legs.
No wonder I
love ice cream.
I never told the truth.

el sueño

As she slept the mother tossed in a mess
of sheets and pillows that waxed into chaos.
A mysterious young man approached her
in a dark alley. He did a lonely dance in the dark

as he sang to the needle and the spoon,
he embraced them with passion.
He ignored the old woman. She sat near
him on the curb as he plunged the needle

hard into his veins. He lifted his starry
upside-down eyes and whispered in her ear,
"I have SIDA. I'm dying. I love you
so much. Lo siento." Then his eyes flipped

right-side-up and the stars fell out as they
overflowed with raindrops of índigo.
They rolled onto the old woman's sleeve and
stained her hanky as she caught them. Her

son fell to his knees. She put her lips
on her son's forehead,
then she noticed her grandfather
sitting silently in the edges of the night.

She heard a thumping, a sound like trying
to tune in a radio station but
there's nothing there—all you hear is *zztzztzzztz*,
static. The hair on her arms stood straight up.

She sighed. The son, mother, and grandfather
fused into one heartbeat that pulsed slower.
The old woman's breathing stopped and all that
could be heard was *zztzztzzztz*.

Mother's Day

The dream dragged her
into the dark.
His arms bandaged
cover up holes.

Weeping, vomiting
in his disgust,
he watches friends die.
It tastes like desire.

Hiding under covers,
using her anger
as a tool, she crawls,
cries on empty, prays.
The piece of her heart
called Mother

dissolves. Tears
roll onto the floor,
out the door,
into the gutter.
He sits on the curb
watches the liquid
heart swirl,
down into colors
of moonlight,
and vanish.

Bilateral Mammogram Dx-Hx
Right Breast Asymmetry

Everyone came to dance on her lawn,
throw their hair back,
let loose, never left her
parties hungry, sad, or drunk.
No one knew why

she had a ten-foot
aspen pole next to her bed.
She came to class one day
minus her long grey braids.
She didn't cry or get angry;

she laughed, rubbed her crew cut
with the palms of her tiny
hands, said she needed a change.
She never missed mom and dad,
like she grieved losing her breast.

No one knew the aspen pole in her
bedroom was the first tree
she ever cut down.
The tree died; she couldn't
burn it, toss it, or forget it.
Like a cancer the roots spread,
new aspen popped up all over
her yard, an aspen grove
with no beginning, no end.

Born Again

You chew nasty mouthfuls of crap.
You'd sell your soul for one pinche
cup of café con leche.
The open window leaks rainfall onto
the bed. You can smell earth and sex.
You'd climb Kilimanjaro for one
puff of a doobie one last, good,
multi-climactic fuck before you kiss
your ass good-bye.
You don't need a priest
or last rites, just one last smoke,
cup of coffee, and fuck.
God in his infinite mercy
supplies morphine-driven dreams
where you screw Juan Valdez
on an enormous, dirty sack of coffee beans.
Afterwards you smoke
some good Columbian mota,
longing for death,
longing to be born again.

Memorial Day

The murdered Mestizos have long been cleared and
begin their new duties as fertilizer for the plantations.

"Bananas" —Lorna Dee Cervantes

The earth is full of dead bodies.
Soon mom will rot in the grave next to dad.
All of mom's friends died.
They knew her playful,

sexy, vicious side.
Mom aches for those days:
she gardened, cooked, chased
children through open meadows,

slow danced with her husband.
She fears sleep, unable to wake
from dreams of rain on green weeds,
steamy vapor clouds. Cool-blue

sky minus shadows.
She grows Mandrágora in her wicked
garden, poison to heal or kill.
In the soft sunset, orange hours,
the dungy earth smolders.

The Aztec Dancers Are Not Aztec

el día de los muertos celebration – Pueblo, Colorado 2007

They call themselves Náhuatl.
At the ceremony drums beat;
my feet dance, no one notices.
The scent of the copal
makes your head melt.
Christians and heathens pray
at altars speckled with sugar skulls
amid crumbs of dead bread.
The very young smile at the very old;
we drink atole, eat pan de los muertos
and tamales because we're traditional.

Some sing songs, some
wish they had sung songs.
Skeletons sell like hot-cakes.
Mujeres dance in skirts tiered in ruffles
like ocean waves of blue foam.
Souls are singing,
"Ana jeyana jeyana jeyo
Ana jeyana jeyana jeyo
Anayana yo anayana yo
Anayana yo anayana yo
Ana jeyana jeyana jeyo."

The Ascension

Sky so blue it hurts.
Trees lean like crosses.
The stream whispers
across soft rocks.

Three mestizos
in blue jeans.
La mujer in the backseat
sees three white men
sunning like snakes
on a slab of red rock.

One man is alone.
He looks like a hippie.
The other two smile;
they're all teeth,
ravenous wolves.

The car slows down – stops.
La mujer opens the door,
stands before the sun,
brilliant blindness, peacock
coloured auras and halos.

The hippie opens his blue eyes:
they are green.
He falls to his knees, hands
raised above his head. He
looks at la mujer sees: Coatlicue,
la virgen, Tonantzin, the Filth Eater.
La mujer roars like a lion.
Her womb blooms
into the heart of the Earth.

rage

all of my friends have been indian
there's a blackfoot in canada
a hopi in arizona   lakota in denver
pawnee in the mountains
and apache on the highway

all of my friends have been indian
we met at a pow wow in the desert
standing in line for fry bread and pop
a bunch of diabetics addicted to sugar and starch
stomachs round   smiles on our stoic faces

all of my friends have been indian
we met auditioning for an indie
indians playing indians
what a concept   we didn't need
hair and make-up   we were shoo-ins

all of my friends have been indians
we met at my brother's funeral   we
stood out among all the suits   women in
fancy designer clothes
we showed up in
jeans t-shirts and sneakers

all of my friends have gone back to their rez
except me   living among the washitu
shape-shifter changing into many things
trickster sneaks like a coyote
waiting waiting

1962

I went to school with white kids
they could always guess my disguise on
halloween 'cause
I was one of two
kids in my class with brown skin   one year
my cuz the stick and I decided
to switch places
he dressed in drag for the first time at ten
and I came as john wayne
I tried so hard to fool the teacher
the students   myself
in the end no one was fooled   so I vowed to try harder
I've been playing dress up and pretend ever since

grandmother sang songs and told stories as if
her life depended on it
her husband drank anyway
she tried to acculturate by reading the
bible and singing hymns

grandfather ran out of money
and ran out of time
he left on purpose to
save her from the truth
the truth that he was an indian

2001

I wish I knew where grandfather's buried because
I'd sing for him and burn sage and sweet grass
and tell him that I forgive him for leaving us
he was having too much fun being Indian

LOS HOMBRES

The Hat

for Julian Aragón 1917-1992

My Dad died broke as the day he was born.
We had to pass the hat to bury him.
He would have been so embarrassed,
pero he spent every nickel he made
taking care of his ten children.
I didn't get an inheritance from my Dad.
He left me his hat.
It sits in the back window of my Chevy.
It hangs there getting sun-bleached and dusty.
It's a cowboy hat, stained with his sweat,

slate grey, leather band, dull brass buckle,
It's a working hat.
The dust and dirt of the milpa cling to the hat.
I plant kernels of corn on his hat;
they sprout. It's a corn hat.
Dad loved the feel of the dirt in his hands,
the smell of the freshly worked soil,
the melody of a bird devouring
freshly turned worms
in rows of ripe red tomatoes.

He loved rain, snow, wind, sunshine.
I can see him bent over, toiling in the garden,
soaking up the sun, tanning his back
to a golden café con leche.
He never wore a shirt,
but he wore that hat.

•

Dad strolls down Fourth Street
his lunchbox swings by his side.
We race to meet him
push and shove each other.
I'm the first one
to get the treat he'd save
for the fastest runner.
He'd wake at three-thirty
in the morning;
we slumbered in our chonies.

He'd put on his hat
and head out the door
feed the chickens, gather eggs,
cook some huevos rancheros
con papas y tortillas,
then he'd make his lunch,
with the dessert he never ate,
(sweets were treats saved for us)
and catch his ride to work.
Under the hat, his full head of

wavy salt and pepper hair,
eyes the color of root beer,
alabaster skin,
except where the sun kissed it
cocoa-brown like
the dirt he cultivated,
brown like the freckles
that covered his rosy cheeks;
brown like mine.

Dad would bite into a raw onion
eat it like an apple and tell me,
"I never had no stinkin' cold
or been to the doctor."
He died an old man.
All ten of his children gathered,
watching the machines
breathe for him.
He grabbed my arm,
pulled me close to his face,

locked eyes with me,
no words. But I knew.
It's our secret.

I treasure the last hat he wore;
Old Spice and a life
of hard work still lingers.
I wore the hat to his funeral.
Down the hill for miles,
car after car, people stood
elbow to elbow, men and women cried
during taps and the twenty-one-gun salute.
In my dreams
he's wearing that hat:
He is ten years old,
drives cattle for rico ranchers
in the canyons, smiles at the Colorado sun.

Dad is a young man
with dark curly hair,
a strong muscular body dressed
in his baseball cap
and uniform on the mound;
his eyes sparkle
like rain on a tin roof
with a laugh like music
the gold tooth in his smile;
pencil mustache,

his big mestizo nose,
my nose.
Miners play inmates
inside the walls of Old Max,
Dad bends his knees,
leans forward,
looks down home plate
at the angry
man in prison stripes.
Dad hurls a pitch,

strikes him out,
strikes out the next man and the next.
He is a Chicano Sailor dressed in white.
His dark skin and light eyes glisten
like the Pacific's hot waves.
He survives WWII but not poverty,
returns a hero
but not to the priest who curses,
flings Dad's pennies
across the church,

"I don't want your dirty pennies!"
Dad signed the cross, put on his hat,
left the church, never returned. He fed
his children love and tortillas in his home,
a sanctuary: his garden an oasis.
He grew corn, chile, tomatoes, raised ten
children of the sun, loved us more than
God, the church, the priest.
When kids yelled at me,
"Hey, you dirty Mexican,"

and called me a lesbo, he'd tell me,
"Hijita, you know who you are,
hell with them." Dad was ambidextrous,
feminine and masculine, yin and yang,
his head high, shoulders back
like a man worth millions,
but he'd pull out his wallet
shake out only lint.
I'm not a cowboy or a cowgirl;
I'm the exact opposite.
I'll be a little old lady wearing that hat,
The crazy vieja wearing the hat.

el día de los muertos

Then he said, "Let me show you something."
And led me to the kitchen,
took out flour, salt, lard, and made masa.
He began to knead it with his ancient,
calloused hands,
hands that had worked
in the fields forty years already.

He threw the tortilla into the air;
it landed on the griddle,
like magic browned,
first yellow then darker with white speckles.
He flipped it in the air back and forth
between his hands and whispered: "Hot, hot, hot!"
It smelled and tasted like love.

One time he gave me a kiss on the cheek
so light that the kiss spirited around
the world and returned
many years later to surprise me.

I built an altar with sugar skulls,
photographs of Dad,
las calaveras dressed in sombreros,
huaraches, red, green and white sarapes.
They danced, played flutes and guitars.
One was dressed like a bride, one as a groom.
The crepe flowers were the wind.
Candles lit the dark way for the spirits.
Sage and sweet grass smoldered.
La virgen de Guadalupe held out her hands,
her blue robe splashed with the moon and the stars,
at her feet, red roses.
Center stage sat a glass of beer,
bowl of frijoles, green chile, and a tortilla.
I celebrated death; I danced with los muertos.
I honored the old ways.

Perfecto

Villa Nueva, New México 1927

Rocks crumble into tired red sand;
the earth spins, arroyos and mesas
plummet and fall. The Pecos River
laughs through the valley
lush with orchards.

No one speaks English;
no one hears the screams
of the dead.
Disease slow dances,
asks for a refund,

demands silent lungs.
Spanish priests chant,
light candles, and dream.
Dust drifts about, looks for salvation.
Children fear breathing;

hold hands and pray.
Now the sky rains rosaries
that fill pockets with doubt.
The geraniums cry
into the collection basket,
turn the pesos small and filthy.
Pears rot in the cocina;
they thirst for fresh air.
Perfecto runs down the street
in his red underwears

screaming, "Viva Perfecto!
Viva Perfecto!"
The tortillas are burning,
the scent is like murder,

black eyes look like questions,

teeth fall onto your
tongue and sizzle.
Mi abuela whispers in my ear,
"Living is easy.
It's the dying that's hard."

The Ninth-Annual Abbey Mardi Gras Celebration

Priests with whiskey breath
smoke cigars, drive big Caddies
to the liquor store,
and buy cigarettes and booze.
Nuns kneel, not to pray;
they scrub woodwork
with toothbrushes.

Monks stroll piously
through the courtyard;
They whip their rope belts
like lariats.

Belly dancers line up
at the stop sign,
the fork in the road,
wonder which way to go;
left, right, straight.
Their bellies
hang dangerously
over their little transparent
scarves with golden bells.
When they sneeze they tinkle.

The chef pedals up
whizzes by on his bike. He
knows which way to go,
never straight. He's masculine,
with perky but hard as rocks breasts,
wears Cleopatra eyeliner;
his hair in a tight bun;
he parks his bike,
swishes in the "out" door
of the kitchen.

The church ladies
burn the main course,
make a collective sigh
of relief, as the she-man
waltzes in and takes charge.

The belly dancers
set up to rehearse,
crank the music
over the intercom,
flood the entire
grounds with
Middle-Eastern music.

The monks
shake their hips, saunter
toward their cells;
nuns hum along, clean
the floors on their hands and knees.

The sheriff arrives
in a cloud of dust at his heels.
He jingles his spurs,
smiles and shimmies
over to the chef who winks, drops his
apron, then gets dipped
over the ice machine.

The meanest, ugliest
gunfighter alive
cha-chas in the front door,
draws both six-shooters and blasts
the fat belly dancer;
she drops to the floor
kind of writhes, spins, giggles.

Big balloons bounce about,
beads, ribbons, laughter

hang from the Catholic rafters.
Étouffée, gumbo, and jambalaya
waft the air.

The high school thespians
electric slide across
the hardwood floors;
(they smoked some mota
and have quite a buzz on.)

The chicks dress Goth
and the dudes a mix of afros,
70's bell bottoms,
head bands,
tie dyed t-shirts,
fringe suede jackets.
The Goth girls look like
vampires; the hippie boys
like the Grateful Dead.

The church bells toll
five o'clock, supper time.
The monks, nuns, priests, cooks
strut into the room.

Vampires dance with nuns;
belly dancers shove
their monstrous boobs
in the faces of inebriated priests.
Flame feathers, skull face,
black with large teeth,
New Orleans magic-chaos.
Shocked eyebrows green,
long pins poked in your doll.
The pain feels so nasty, delicious.
Witchy wisdom burnt with matches,
candles melt — so do you.

Just a Man

In the square of the churchyard,
squinting at the blazing sun
in his white cowboy hat,
black robe, priest's collar,
hands clasped in front of him,
he stands stoic, poised, regal, calm.
He visits a burn center,
an AIDS clinic, an orphanage,
el barrió, the mill, the fields.
His immaculate presence, posture,
his little mustache and goatee
sculpted, lips luscious, eyes inviting.

The man of God
generates sexuality, chastity:
el Chicano, el indio, el hombre,
flesh and bone, human, not Saint
not sinner: Just a man.

Desire   lust   dreams   naked   women
big chi chis cha cha
onto his huge altar.
Man of the cloth—
celibate — sacrifice.
Latino man with no mojo.
Wishes the missionaries
stayed in Española
he could've been just another
vato loco in Tenochtitlan
gettin' his groove on.

Diego García Island of Secrets

Manuel, that man with the heart,
lusts for Maravilla, her name
like missiles launched.
Sun burnt henna hair
velvet-satin eyes,
skin soft with submission.

That isle of hot winds and
rain like bullets.
Moonlight girls dance
with dank men, smashed on paradise,
lava liquor, sinful barbeques,
sandy white lies.

Isle of pirates, equator
shifts to conga beat,
coconut and donkey worship.
Earthquake dances like sparks,
sharks dive, Philippines shimmied alive.
Girls climb in windows whisper sex,
dare to dance on top of fire.
The dangerous sea shell
waters sting, hot eyes.
Desert Storm soldiers sing
cuentos of revolucíon.

Intercultural Competence
or Why I Married a White Man

for Vincent

Your aura, like Gabriel's
        so bright it blazed
and blinded.
            The hurt healed my ache.
Your love absolved my sins.

La luna absurda
y desesperada
ebbs with the tears of blood.
Lies are beginning
to climb downwards.

You remember my memories.
Save me from me.
Listening to your
sweet screams
brings possibilities.

You came to my party
in a black leather jacket
looking very 80's in the 90's,
bad teeth and cigarette breath,
your smile shy and lacking ego,

met your first drag queen,
kissed her hand gently,
never flinched; your green eyes
flamed star-like at me.

In the kitchen standing strong
over the sink you asked my father
permission to marry his daughter,
the two of you laughed;
I knew you were just like him:

Your Libra scales of justice
unable to make a decision,
you decided on me
even though I had a crummy job,
no dowry, and no tiny waist.

You sing "Girls Just Wanna Have Fun"
out-of-key at the top of your lungs,
hate homophobic racists,
can't dance or dress yourself,
but you move rocks for me.

Even though we have five cats,
you want more.
You are neither a chauvinist
nor a feminist.
You are that new breed of man
that wears my faded "CHICANA,"
"Mestiza," or "Lady Saigon" t-shirts.
It tickles you that I cuss like a sailor
and lead on the dance floor.
You run into the kitchen
to cry during chick flicks,
laugh your ass off to mask your sobs.
You are handsome as a man.
But as a human you are beautiful.

Two-Spirit

Les, my brother,
was walking
with two bags
full of groceries,
a gallon of milk.
He stood at the red light
trying to decide,
"Should I cross the street;
should I stay here
and wait and see?"
I turned on my left blinker,

the light turned green;
I gave it gas,
headed straight for him
before he could blink.
He probably thought
I was mad at him,
he always says,
"You hate me don't you sis?"
Probably thought
I was going to
give him a drive by;

run his ass over.
I pulled up, said, "Hop in."
He looked at me with disbelief,
pulled up his pants,
opened the door and stumbled
into my '73 Pontiac LeMans.
I gave him a ride today.
Dropped him off to drink
himself to death or worse.
I got home; the answering

machine was mad.
It blinked at me

with a fiery red eye.
I pushed the red eye;
it spoke to me.
Another brother needed a ride.
A ride to salvation.
I took my dog for a walk,
laughed at the clouds.
One brother drinks
himself to death
and carries a gallon of milk.
Another bro bums a ride to jail
to do work release,

so he can send child
support to his girls on the rez.
Les sits at home and wonders
why his crack-head wife
never comes home.
Why his daughter
looks just like him,
but his wife swears
he isn't the father.
My brother in drag
throws a drag,

drags on a joint,
drags his ass around town
in drag, wears miniskirts
shows off beautiful, tan legs.
The guys all whistle.
He's only a woman on the inside.
The curse of being born hairy,
big boned, with an Adam's apple.

He cooks, bakes, cleans house
just like a housewife,
but who would ever

marry this Two-Spirit?
Who would ever settle
down in his house
with a white picket fence
and raise children with him?
He used to steal,
promised he would never
steal from me again.
Never steal my credit card,
my money, my husband.
But, then again, he lies too.

Myth of the Boogey Man

The Maya and Inca dreamed of the monster,
the demon named Pusilánimos.
The Mayan warrior went into the quag to quell
the noise of the deep. He became raw, had a
rapt fever for feeding on the dead.
He began to rack and ravish their bones.
He sucked and sapped their piquant blood
to quaff his thirst for blood.
Ate a sapid brew of meat and skin to sate his depravity.
He devoured their children
became el Cuycuy.

GARDEN OF EDEN

The Garden of Eden

The sun sets, pale
white flowers bloom,
warm midnight autumn
breeze kisses the nape of
my neck.
You cut my braids,
silver locks fall
past the ghost of my breast.
Children wear
fifty-year old braids.
Recycled
beauty,
recycled death.

At Wind River

New México 2006

I picked up the stone lying in the mud:
milk quartz made of minerals,
created from sun heat,
the cool nights. It is alive,
an element of the universe,
facet of God.
It sat on top of muck,
white on black.

Energized by the stone of the sun,
wind, rocks, trees;
I turned childlike — passionate,
evolved, more spiritual,
gracious. At Wind River
I learned religion of nature,
not man.

Aloe

Lizard-like emerald blades of Netherlands and Antilles,
their limbs grow in every direction like yucas and puyas
across the mouth of the river of sand. Sharp, pointed,
alligator leaves gorged with nature's remedies.
Bitter-sweet, sticky, slime,
medicine of Anasazi.

Their octopus tendons grow heavy
and burst succulent dew,
an oasis of moisture to quench;
gods, you store rain in these vessels.
Perfect in design,
they collect for centuries and never fear drought.

Killers

They have survived through evolution.
Exotic and perilous with
fierce, bright colors, spikes that kill,
sticky, hairy, bristled, claw-like,
slippery flutes envelope, suffocate,
dissolve soft parts leaving only
remnants, tiny skeletons.
It's illegal to hunt Pinguicula in Grand Marais.
Development threatens them.

Creepy, hungry, carnivorous Sundew
Nepenthes Truncata
live in humid jungles their lethal traps
snap shut, the victim drowns in digestive
juices—fungi consumes
amoebas in the Sax-Zim bog.

In wetlands
full of pretty flowers the quarry
can't escape. Morticia's Cleopatra,
a Venus Freak
with her glistening foliage
lures vertebrates to their demise.
Even propagated tissue cultures
in suburbs kill.
Nature ventures to adapt.

The Rain

My spirit in decay,
washed in London rain,
Lear's tears and dreams
realize, visualize deception, lies,
forgive mothers, remember
fathers, tremble in churches,
fall to your knees.

Othello suffocates Desdemona;
the fool teaches truths to Kings
who weep naked, die laughing,
on words, words, words.

Tithing Ten Percent

And I will make thy seed to multiply as the stars of the heaven, and will give unto thy seed all these countries; and in thy seed shall all the nations of the earth be blessed . . .

—Genesis 26.4

Grandfather, full-blooded Navajo,
four-year-old orphan
sold by Utes to a Mexican in Alamosa
for food and a horse.
Sheepherder, miner, migrant worker,
he dug, tilled, tended; loved the land,
spread seeds, grew children,
and planted truths.

•

Grandmother put on a clean apron
everyday stoked the fire,
cracked an egg, and put the shells in the pot
to keep coffee grounds
from rising to the top.
She rolled tortillas,
served frijoles and chile,
kissed her children goodbye.
Sat on the porch in her rocker,
reached in her apron pocket,
for tobacco and paper,
and rolled her smokes.
She sat and she rocked.
Rock of ages cleft for me,
let me hide myself in thee.

My parents learned hunger,
how to pray, *Forgive me Father, for I have sinned.*
Mom stole bologna and beans.
The store owner looked the other way,
bagged her groceries,
loved her for feeding her children.
He cried when she died –
placed lilacs on her grave.

•

My father gave pennies for his tithe,
The priest threw them at my father,
"Stupid Mexican! I don't have
time to count your damn pennies!"
The priest broke Dad's heart.

In St. Mary's, Dad refused last rites,
surrounded by ancestors,
los muertos, los espíritus,
ten stalks of golden maíz.
He smiled and died.
Bendito, bendito, bendito, sea Dios,
Los ángeles cantan y alaban a Dios,
Los ángeles cantan y alaban a Dios.

•

My parents ate their
cereal with water,
saved the milk for us.
Dad drove an old truck, cut lawns,
trimmed trees, raked leaves. Mom ironed,
washed, scrubbed other people's clothes.
My parents ate beans, beans, and more beans,
they broke their backs in fields for us.